scream before they kill your poetry

© 2018 Pete Donohue
© Cover Art: 2018 Pete Donohue
Cover design by m7chelle@gmail.com

49 /50

Published and Edited by
John D Robinson
Holy&intoxicated Publications: UK:

ISBN: 978-1-78926-929-1

Dedicated to

Tania, Finn and Clover.

Acknowledgements:

Special thanks to all the spoken word platforms, litzines and independent publishers who believe in my work and continue to support it. Also a big thank you to all involved at www.hastingsindependentpress.co.uk

Author biog:

Irish-born and London-raised **Pete Donohue** works in community mental health in amazing Hastings on the Dirty South Coast of a proudly multi-cultural England and preserves his dubious sanity through creative writing, drawing, editing, reviewing and performing poetry, short stories and music.

Twitter: @petedonohuepoet

Contents

scream

we stay together

pigeons talk to me

coming down together

crossword corner

bad genes

carcrash

lifelong goddess

fool's gold dance

meat school vegan

drink

property & theft

deep

rip

kick back girl

the next bag

the honey & whiskey graveyard

scream

there may
have been one
when i slipped
shrivelled & wet
from the uterus
into this
dangerous world
how would i
remember
i do recall
however
later screams
of sibling births
& family frustrations
unable to distinguish
between
those of joy
of surprise
of rebellion
of downright terror
or exclamations
in delight
in frustration
in alarm
in fear of violence
& its aftermath
of pain
& perhaps
a drug comedown
or a eureka
moment
or a vocal
orgasm
maybe
the discovery
of a body
dead
or nearly so
& the incubus

of night sweats
that chokes
all utterances
yet can never
pacify them
until we
slip back
through that
interconnecting
channel
between
the difficulty
of birth
& the ease
of death
to realise
life
is but a scream
until
we know
true
silence.

we stay together

i cup her breast
we scrape bones
slot-slotted together
twin absinthe spoons
drip-drip
sugar cubism rush
faery swirl
la louche engulfs
this thin sheet
shrouds us in
each other's mystery
streaked with urinous
yellow morning
through the blind
the sick the crippled
weak & vulnerable
arms for the pouring
drinks & emotions
alchemical potions
our megahearts beat
together irregularly
stirring stirring
from half-sleep helix
the shudder of love
when truly exchanged
unidentified energies
scream & relax
a coming together
of partial nervous systems
like separate subway lines
adjoined for the journey
district & circle
circle & district
each stop a chance
to draw breath & share
a new destination
my fingers twitch
she strokes them steady
the twist of her lips
pre-raphaelite heaven
her rosehips cushion

my fragile bones
as sunlight stretches
across the room
illuminating ever
new shades of her hair
rivers of copper
silver & gold
each strand a new prospect
glistening with hope
we breathe
we breathe
this future is ours
as it was in the beginning
& together
we own this past
skin to skin
thought to thought
child to adult
we stay together.

pigeons talk to me

it's hot
on the street
with weeds
rampant
swimming
in melting
tarmac
& a wood pigeon
sings
from the canopy
of an overgrown
oak
that blocks
the light
from empty
houses
& destroyed
lives
cooing
hey baby
where you at
i need a fuck
& i can't sing
any louder
than this
or i'll forfeit
all my
sexual energy
& who knows
what else
i may lose
in the course
of my life
so i need
to determine
what is
actually
really
important

before
i die
so come on
over
baby
& make me come
within your
fertile feathers
because we need
more babies
to keep
this fucking tree
alive
to feed
the revolution.

coming down together

with hair a dirt-bomb mess
& tired eyes washed out
she watches as he folds
his angled limbs to press
inventive origami

to grant his ache a stretch
on wine-drenched velvet couch
those veins beneath thin flesh
blue neon flight paths guide
a red mosquito army

within that shallow breath
all layers of a life
intermingle dreamlike
as ripples on the wind
sweep through ripened barley

there will one day come peace
both she & he agree
within these swirls of pain
they still themselves with grace
to live their lives out calmly.

crossword corner

get me out now
of this corner
of the crossword
& this corner
of the house

lost forever
other earthly
bleeding darkness
dim in sunlight
all day long

cold sweat bathing
wrapped in layers
from a world of
fright & torment
all the time

weekday morning
waking nightmares
sleep disturbance
airless breathing
churning guts

pull the blankets
from my body
weakened arms &
nerves in numbness
trembling

swing those bones out
face the window
& the shadow
of this self i
have become

coldrush hit me
burning lungs out
summon up the
night's collection

blood & phlegm

now the nausea
holdback heaving
dizzy washes
icy shivers
warming sweats
pain of coughing
holding hernia
shoulder tension
sharp sciatica
agony

& the itching
fungal scratching
peeling eczema
drawing blood
psoriasis

reach inhalers
drink some water
take a chill pill
stomach porridge
face the day

force the body
into work
& leave the mind
to focus on
the crossword.

bad genes

she had six children
& worked in a zoo
as some kind of specialist
with her biology degree
her eldest son dealt dope
from his bedroom
in her twee house
on the rural outskirts
of hemel hempstead hurts
i knew she didn't like me
or the fact that
i was fucking
her middle daughter
when she said
at the sunday dinner table
give pete more potatoes
he's irish
& when that daughter said
can you give us some money
we want to buy a houseboat
to live together on
her response was
you can't have children
with him
he has a sister with schizophrenia
so i didn't hang around
with her middle daughter
or any of her dysfunctional family
for very much longer
after that.

carcrash

when that car flipped
i saw my life
in slo-mo somersaults
past tense
future tense
only not my
death
it was close to midnight
on the cruel bend
of that fast road
thankfully empty
of other speeding metal
striking out
for the bright lights
of brighton
from the bright lights
of london
i should not have
been driving
& it wasn't even
my car
but the four of us
had this wild idea
my girlfriend sally
in the back with noel
from the croydon pub
my close friend jeremy
in passenger-seat panic
grabbing the wheel
when i had that corner
perfectly under control
like kerouac's cassidy
& then too late
to correct with confidence
as we snaked
into the curb
& rolled over
like a frisky dog
scraping its arse on the tarmac

the crush of the roof
around us
rolling rolling rolling
& then bouncing back
onto four fucked wheels
we four fucked youths
dazed & confused
startled
to be still alive
yet somehow two
doors
could be opened
with a kick
& we all got out
bleeding & staggering
shivering in shock
appreciative of those
who came running
from the big house
when they heard
those sickening noises
of the all-too familiar
misjudgement
of carcrash youth
& those strong irish boys
exiled in england
sons of a sausage-fingered subbie
made good
through cousins & contacts
pub-negotiated contracts
& clever tax avoidance
pushed the wreckage
of that estate car
& ourselves
up the drive
around the back
of the rambling house
hidden from peepers
of traffic squad peelers
where kind mrs rooney
lay on her broken back
holding court
from the sofa

with opioids & brandy
warming us
out of our shock
with bottles
from her bar
as her daughters
dressed our wounds
& gave us
plain cigarettes
no filter tips
before allocating us
rooms for the night
although we were
strangers
with blood
on our hands
& arrogance
on our breath
but such is the way
of hospitable irish
especially in england
where a sense of place
doesn't always make sense
to wild rovers & ramblers
& the next morning
we went to investigate
the remains of last night
& that car
i had borrowed
dizzy with disbelief
when i saw
the violent crush
of all that was left
as i fell to my knees
emptied my guts
onto patio slabs
& marvelled
at the miracle
that we were all
still
alive.

lifelong goddess

it wasn't easy
holding control
as i watched
those beads
of sweat
form
on the suntan
of her breasts
& slip
into rivulets
that converged
in the valley
of her cleavage
beneath intense
theatre lights
as she danced
& sang
sultry
backing vocals
on that low
stage
coloured by
spilt-drink stipple
& dope smoke
wash
but i reined
myself in
although not
on my parade
as i reminded
myself
of the one-woman
man
that i am
with no room
for any other
so i switched
my fantasy
to the one

that i really
love
& worship
so there was
nothing else
left
to do
other than
look forward
to coming home
to my own
faerylights
& my own
true
lifelong
goddess.

fool's gold dance

choose your partner
carefully
as we go dancing
on the hastings
promenade
single file
swing your girl
or your boy
all around
keep your feet
upon the ground
there is a boardwalk
reaching out
across the sea
for you & me
if we can follow
all the fiddles
& resist
the phony shake
of panhandlers
& golden lions
with inflated
ego arrogance
& the smell
of dodgy dealings
could be over
if you dance
in time with our
community
to plainly see
that this fiasco
can't go on.

meat school vegan

not everyone
gets it
this meat school
vegan thing
word association
can be good
or bad
or indifferent
in unequal measures
like punk cocktails
where flavours
meet
but don't
necessarily
compliment
each other
yet deliver
a fuck-you
hit
nonetheless
& meat
is murder
stated morrissey
once
quite obviously
although personally
i always preferred
mark e smith
who never tolerated
pretension
although he tolerated
shitloads
of beer
& speed
as he kept
the vinyl record scene
going
with an energy
& immediacy

unsurpassed
by most
& those
of his ilk
understand
the meaning
of meat school
as an attitude
not a dietary
requirement
or choice
& especially not
a poetry sub-genre
because then
we really would be
falling into
unnecessary
literary classification
which often
turns out
to be
or not to be
bollocks
so let's just say
poetry
is sometimes truth
sometimes raw
sometimes romanticised
sometimes offensive
sometimes
a little bit confused
but so what
if it moves
you
the reader
& me
the writer
then
something
has happened
so let's celebrate
the connection
in whatever way

we choose.

drink

don't drink
to remember
don't drink
to forget
just drink
to be
just drink.

property & theft

i have a house
& a piece
of paper
that says
one day
i will
own
one half
of it
what does
that mean?

it means
i don't
sleep out
on the streets
i have shelter
from bad
weather events
& sociopaths
or parasites

it means
my kids
have a nest
safe from magpies
& groomers
& ruthless fuckers
who turned
the chain gang
into a gang chain
& offer
twisted
family values
with riches
thrown in
at a price
none of us
can really

afford.

deep

i go deep
it's dark here
no light
to blind me
no saviour
shuttering
my soul
i go deep
it's dark.

rip

he shared my name
was a bit older
had a punk
teddy boy thing
going on
always in black
subtle quiff
sideburns
drape
drainpipes
winkles
the cramps
his favourite band
along with
the clash
his hands
always in
his pockets
we lived together
for a while
in the crazy flat
at the mansions
twelve rebels
a dirty dozen
each with a different
beef
although we were
all vegetarians
& drug fiends
each
of individual
preferences
& particularities
he lost his sister
like i did
(later)
& his mother
(a teacher)
at the same time

a dreadful car crash
when he was
still
a teenager
he never talked
about it
to me
but i knew
all the details
from others
he had
the smallest
room
in the flat
a single bed
for him
& loose
his soulmate
& blood sister
who often
stopped by
& one day
when the dealer
had left
he told me
yes
i have a
small habit
but it's no
problem
i had to
take him
at his word
& the next year
we were all drinking
at a local pub
& i knew
he was high
& he said
i have to go
& he went
to his car
the one

his father
the only remaining
member of his family
had given him
it was parked outside
the pub
where he fell
asleep behind
the wheel
before
he could even
start it up
& when we
came out
we saw him
non compos mentis
in a fug
semi-comatose
& tried to
pull him
out of it
like we were
jump leads
connecting our batteries
to his
but it was
no good
& he told us
to go away
so we left
& later
the police came
& breathalysed him
even though
he wasn't even
driving
but that was the end
of his licence
& his car
& a few years
further on
down the line
he had moved

to a different
flat
& headspace
where i stayed
& wrote
a country blues
through the night
to play him
at dawn
on his old
battered
semi-acoustic
with rusty strings
& he said
i could have
written that
so i said
yeah
but you didn't
did you
which was when
i knew
he had given up
& a couple years
later
i got the phone call
to say
he was dead
three days
before they found him
in his favourite
armchair
the needle
still
in his own
arm.

kick back girl

i laid my soul
on the line
for him
but he really
fucked
with my head
all my good
intentions
sucked up
by a psychic
vampire
no wonder
i came home
every night
after work
& took
multiple pulls
on the vodka
& the spliffs
& strange cocks
& unsettled sanity
until all options
were exhausted
& I fell
into realisation
that life
is for living
oneself
& not
to let others
succeed
in putting
the boot in
because i
can kick too
only harder.

the next bag

she knocked
on my door
i need a fiver
she told me
for a bag
all right
what happens
if i don't
cough up
i wondered
then i'll smash
a car window
& get it
that way
she said
don't do that
i shook
my head
you might hurt
yourself
i worried
she laughed
you know
i'm hurt
already
but glass
i argued
you could cut
yourself
so what
she scoffed
i ain't no
haemophiliac
i've just got
hep c
i'm hiv negative
it ain't no
big deal
i scratched

my balls
& my head
she had beautiful
panda eyes
i gave her twenty
please
don't die
i begged
she pulled her face
into the closest
she could get
to a smile
& was gone.

the honey & whiskey graveyard

you are the honey & i am the whiskey
together we mingle with spices & citrus
dissolved in each other's bespoke hot water
we float as if smoke in our lovers' quarter

following swarmways of bees in adventure
weak at the knees distraught to the senses
nurturing feelings to keep us alive
swirling like king & queen of the hive

the reach of those fingers won't let me alone
as breath from your whisper enriches my bones
i scream out desire at the lilt of your name
with you at my side i am free of all pain

the dance of your eyes conjures music of angels
a spark in your smile to celebrate strangeness
you radiate cool with acceptance & passion
a casual demeanour dictating high fashion

i learnt long ago never dwell on dissent
simply meet middleways or else walk off & vent
we need to be loved from the heart of another
our own special person plus sisters & brothers

such depth of emotion engenders confession
clean sweeps of our conscience ensure redemption
the gift of your presence refreshes my soul
we are childlike as adults despite growing old

forgive me my sins they were never intended
whatever was lost is no longer defended
i can't let you go for even one moment
each shape of your absence will haunt me with torment

through staggering walkways we strolled out together
where stepping-stone stars can unite us forever
for once i have loved you a myriad of ways
magnolia roots shall encircle my grave.